I Remember...

I Remember...

Memories of
Growing Up

Kevin Kammeraad

a **Tomato** Collection book

I remember the day at Joe's when I didn't quite make it
to the bathroom on time;
we were playing outside when it happened.
I didn't quite know what to do,
but once I got inside the bathroom,
I threw my underwear into the bathtub
and closed the curtain.
I knew nobody would find them there!
(Or at least nobody would know whose they were.)

Mrs. Dorgelo found them that same day.
I was the only kid in the household who wore that
size underwear.

I was a little embarrassed.

*****

Every morning before school I would wake up early.
I'd get my cereal and turn on the TV.
"Do, do, do, do, do..." went the opening.

That crazy inspector,
he never knew anything;
it was always Penny and the dog saving the day.
And never,
never,
did they show that bad guy's face.
But I kept watching,
thinking maybe someday,
someday they'll show his face.

Day after day,
I would eat my cereal,
watch the show,
and then head off to school.

Eventually (I don't remember when),
I stopped watching *Inspector Gadget*.
I never did see "the face."

*****

I was a pretty clever kid.
I had my room set up so I could turn on my light
right from my bed.
Here's how:
I tied a string to my light switch
and covered it with a little bit of tape.
I then ran the string straight up to the ceiling to the hook
I had put there.
The string went across the ceiling,
over to another hook above my bed,
down the wall,
and hung by the side of the bed.
With one pull of the string,
the light was on.
It was quite the set up.

I never did, however,
figure out a clever way to turn *off* the light.

*****

Every night,
Mom would read a story to me.
When we were finished,
we'd pray,
and then she would kiss me good night.
She would turn off the lamp and then leave the room.

One day,
I became old enough to read and pray on my own.
That was the end of stories with Mom.

*****

On the back of our house there was a faucet.
Joe and I would turn on the faucet and let the water run.
Since the backyard at that time was only sand,
we would carve a path,
and the backyard would become a river.

Some days,
we would build a reservoir with a dam that we could
quickly break,
filling our riverbed with rushing water.

I think this river kept us busy for an entire summer.

*****

Every summer,
Grandma and I used to go up to her cottage just to mow
the lawn and clean up a bit.
Years before,
the cottage was a busy place,
but I don't remember those days.
What I remember is Grandma and I going there mostly
to maintain it.

When we would pull into the driveway,
we'd gasp at the knee-deep lawn and the weeping willow
that shed over the grass.
Usually, I would mow and Grandma would rake.

In the neighbors' backyard,
there was an old water pump.
I was usually in charge of getting the water.
I'd walk over with a bucket in hand,
set it under the pump,
and fill it up.

After a long day,
we would relax inside the cottage.
In the back,
there were two rooms
and a closet with a small portable potty.

The first bedroom,
which was Grandma's room,
had a small dresser.
In the bottom drawer were markers,
crayons,
and odds and ends.
I don't remember what was in the second room.

At night,
I would sleep on the sofa;
it had bumpy, blue fabric.

When it was time to leave,
the last thing to be done was to empty the portable potty
into the full-size portable potty down by the lake.
I never did like that part.

Even though I don't remember the cottage much during
its prime,
the memories with only Grandma and me are just as good.

*****

Joe and I loved to jump on the trampoline.
(It was best at night.)
We would each have a wet washcloth in one hand;
I would be on one side,
he on the other.
On three,
we'd throw our cloths into the air and fall on our backs.
One of us would be catapulted a mile high.
The goal: to catch the cloth.
Usually, I would be the one who flew highest.
(It was because Joe was heavier than I,
but that's another story.)
We loved that game.

Another thing we often did was play in the creek behind
Pastor Phil's house.
One day,
Joe's foot got caught in an animal trap.
I ran to his house as fast as I could.
"Mrs. Dorgelo! Mrs. Dorgelo!
Joe's caught in a bear trap!"
His dad, mom, and I walked back to the creek
in no big hurry.
(I couldn't understand why they weren't more concerned
about a bear trap.)

Once we arrived,
Mr. Dorgelo easily pried open the trap,
and we all walked back to their house.
I guess it wasn't as bad as I thought.

I also remember Joe's brother had the greatest posters in
his room.

*****

One Christmas morning,
I woke everyone up at 7 a.m. by playing my trumpet.
I think I played *Jingle Bells*.

*****

Andy and I were born only a couple of months apart.
He lived across the street and we did everything together.
That all changed when my family moved the summer after
I was in Kindergarten.
I was upset about it,
but every so often I was able to sleep over at his house,
or he'd sleep over at mine.

One time,
when I was staying at his house,
it was getting pretty late.
I realized that we might be up until midnight;
I had never stayed up that late before.
I got excited because my digital watch showed the date,
and I had always wanted to see it change.

I did,
and then we went to sleep.

I guess simple things entertained me back then.

*****

We built our new house in Holland the summer after
I graduated from Kindergarten.
I remember pounding in a few nails.
As we built the house,
we lived with Grandma,
where Dad grew up.
Mom and Dad slept in the basement;
Kristi, Lori, and I slept upstairs.
I was in Dad's old room,
while Kristi and Lori shared Aunt Diane's.

I always had a tough time getting to sleep at night.
It was because little people lived in the walls of that room,
(or so I thought).
I could see their tiny faces,
especially when the moon shined into the room.

I remember waking up one night and having to pee,
but I didn't dare move.
If I did,
those little people might get me.
"Lori! Kristi!" I yelled.
I yelled for quite some time.
Eventually, Lori walked into the room.
(It must have been her turn.)
"I have to pee," I said.
Lori escorted me downstairs,
then waited in the hall to take me back up.

Today,
no one sleeps in those bedrooms except when relatives
come in from out of town.
I wonder if the knotted pine walls scare them at night?

*****

She only came to Michigan a few times,
but when she did,
my cousin Jade and I made the best spook houses.
We were quite the team.
We made them in Grandma's basement,
in the room with the pool table.

Once everything was set and planned,
Grandma, Aunt Diane, Sapphire, and anyone else available
would be our guests.
If Jade was the guide,
I would be in charge of each "station."
Vice versa.

We would lead our guests in a circle around the pool table,
and then back out.
(It wasn't a very long spook house.)
The best part was always the mysterious flashing light in
the washing machine.
Grandma never did find out how we did that.

*****

I remember playing softball in Cub Scouts.
We had green T-shirts.
Once,
I said something mean to Nate during a game.
I don't remember what it was,
but I've felt bad ever since.
Maybe it didn't even hurt his feelings,
and I'm sure he has long forgotten,
but I've felt bad ever since.

I'm sorry Nate.

*****

Grandma used to be in a band with old ladies
who dressed up in funny costumes.
They played songs using homemade instruments
and often visited rest homes to play their music.
It was kind of goofy,
but that's what made it so interesting.
Sometimes, I went along with her.
I blew bubbles during certain songs,
I carried stuff in and out,
and I did other things to help.

Joe came along with us once.
That day,
while Grandma was setting up,
we walked into the dining room
and were stopped by a very old lady who wanted to say
hello or something.
Since we couldn't understand what she said,
we didn't know what to say in response.

We did understand, however, when she looked at Joe
and congratulated him on being pregnant.

Neither Joe nor I knew what to say as we stood there
with a half smile.

These days, Joe's a skinny guy.

*****

I used to make a squeaky noise with my mouth.
Eventually, I was able to pronounce words in that "voice."
I could say,
"Oh, boy."
"Uh-oh."
"I don't know."
"Bye-bye."
"Oh, well."
It was pretty neat.
I did it quite a bit.

One day,
Mom and Dad said I had to give them a quarter every time I did it.
That was a pretty clever idea on their part.

*****

It was very common that after school I had to run off the bus and hurry home because I *really* had to use the bathroom. One time,
I flew into the house,
straight into the bathroom,
and found Lori's friend Heather sitting on the toilet hollering, "I'm in here!"

Oops.

*****

My friend Mike and I used to play outside a lot.
In the back of his house there was a creek.
We would often try to catch minnows or other small fish,
swim in it,
and sometimes even build bridges across it.
In front of the creek there was a hill.
On one part of the hill,
above the swamp,
there was a rope.
We'd swing above the swamp and hope we didn't fall off.
In the winter,
we'd go sledding all day on the hill and try not to end up
in the creek.

Behind our house,
a little ways back,
there was a huge pile of trees.
(They had been cut down because a small power plant
was built where the trees used to stand.)
That pile of trees was an undiscovered island to us,
and we made sure to claim it!
We had forts, tunnels, bomb shelters,
and even a lookout point.
Hours seemed like minutes when we were there.

When Mike and I got together, we were never bored.

*****

Every year,
our family would go camping in Ludington.
Every year.
The campground had a nature center;
I loved to go there and push buttons on the boxes.

I remember lots of trails,
a river with a brown bridge,
a dam that always had "rain,"
a candy store,
and lots of people fishing.
(I never caught much myself.)

One year,
Dad and I decided we would go camping,
just the two of us.
Instead of Ludington, however,
we went to the Upper Peninsula.
On the first night,
the mosquitoes drove us nuts.
We decided to move to another campground.

The new place was right on the lake,
and there was a cliff that went down to the beach.
I remember the sunset was incredible that night.

The next day while hiking,
we saw a deer run past us.
We kept walking and came upon a baby fawn
lying in the path,
barely old enough to stand.
Slowly,
she raised herself up on her feeble legs and stared at us.
Dad took a picture.

I think I'll always remember that trip.
I'll remember hiking through all the trails.
I'll remember those pesky mosquitoes.
I'll remember that little fawn with big ears.
Mainly, I'll remember hanging out with Dad.

*****

Grandpa and Grandma had the greatest pool.
I'd swim and swim (and swim).

I remember Brian and I would try to swim underwater all
the way across the pool without taking a breath.
(The flippers helped.)

I remember...the little door that sucked in toys.

...the small, blue tub of water where we had to wash the
grass off our feet before going in.
It was just big enough to fit both feet.

...rolling the pool cover on and off.
It looked like that bubble-packing-stuff in boxes.

...when the blue slide was added,
complete with a turn in the middle.
We'd go down on our bellies, butts, backs,
you name it.

...mowing the lawn across the street - every Tuesday.
Mrs. Kline would leave the $10 under the rug.
Afterwards,
I'd go for a swim and then play cards with Grandma.
I'd usually win,
but she never gave up.
While we played,
we ate cookies out of the small tin box.

...having to put a plastic bag over my cast in first grade.

...goofing around underwater with a mask on.
It was fun to grab people's feet.

Grandpa and Grandma had the greatest pool.

*****

I remember piling in the car after church,
turning on to Butternut Drive,
and stopping at Mother Hubbard every Sunday.
Dad would come back with the Sunday paper
and a candy bar – the Hershey Big Block.
Kristi, Lori, and I would each get a piece.
(It conveniently came in three break-apart pieces.)

When we would get home,
Lady would be waiting by the door.

*****

Joe's mom made the best snack.
It was a bowl of bananas,
milk,
and sugar on top.

One day I asked her for the recipe.

*****

29

My Great Grandfather had Alzheimer's disease.
I only knew him when he wasn't really "living."
Most of the time he was in bed.

I remember visiting every Sunday night
and never enjoying *Murder She Wrote* at 8 p.m.
I remember their trailer home,
the marble coffee table,
and the candy dish with the pink and white peppermints.
I remember the day when Kristi and Lori split the small
carton of milk.
(It was coffee cream.)
I remember the slippers Great Grandpa wore on his feet.
(They were actually the liners from winter boots.)

One day their trailer was sold,
and Great Grandma and Grandpa moved in with Grandma.
(We lived next door.)

Often,
Dad would sit on the foot stool next to Great Grandma.
She would rub his back while he read the paper
and talked with her.
We all sat on that foot stool from time to time.
When I sat at the stool,
I'd hear stories of how Great Grandpa was a wonderful
band director and teacher.
(I used his trumpet when I was in band.)

I'll never forget the night dad woke me up,
"Great Grandpa passed away," he said quietly.

I was too scared to go over there,
but the rest of the family went.

*****

One weekend when I was in Kindergarten,
there was a garage sale across the street.
Kenny, a kid from down the block,
and I were playing outside;
we decided to go check it out.
I don't remember exactly what it was we found,
but we both wanted it.
It was some sort of toy,
and I remember that it was really something great.
The sticker on it read: $1.
We looked at each other for a second,
and then we both ran home with a single mission: $1.
"Mom, Mom! I need a dollar! Quick!"
I didn't have time to explain.
"Please!"

I don't remember the exact details of whether or not I
got the dollar,
but I remember going back to the garage sale
and seeing Kenny handing his dollar to the woman.

Noooooo...!

*****

I don't remember where we were,
maybe at somebody's cottage,
but I do remember a lake.
Many people were there as well as lots of food.
I was busy playing when Mom came running up to me
frantically apologizing.
"For what?" I must have asked.
It turns out that my family had left without me.
(It's not as if they drove for hours laughing hysterically
that their plan had worked. They were only gone a few
minutes; I hadn't even noticed.)

I can imagine, however,
that Kristi and Lori must have tried their best to keep
from laughing.

*****

I remember finding out I was going to have Mr. Feenstra
instead of Mrs. Robertson for my fifth grade teacher.
I was disappointed,
but only because Lori had Mrs. Robertson and said she
was really nice.

My desk was near the back of the classroom,
and I sat right next to the wall.
On my left was a long row of books,
and one day I picked up *Henry and his Dog*.
It was a good book.
I went on to read more books about Henry,
then some about Ralph S. Mouse,
and some others about a girl named Ramona.

I used to go to the room down the hall and practice how
to pronounce the difference between "th" and "s."
They fixed the problem.

One day,
Mr. Feenstra and our class discussed this statement:
"No grass grows under my feet."
I didn't understand it.
Why did the grass stop growing?
I also remember the day I finally understood it.

On April Fools' Day,
Marcus said he lost his voice.
He made it the *entire* day without talking.

Every Friday we had the choice of white or chocolate.
I always chose chocolate.
If we had hot lunch,
we walked to the kitchen to get our tray,
then returned to our classroom to eat.
I usually had hot lunch.

Fifth grade was a pretty good year.
(I ended up liking Mr. Feenstra.)

*****

After school,
I would often make sandwiches -
usually two or three.
I would use two slices of white bread
and exactly three slices of lunch meat.
I'd put my three slices of lunch meat on my bread
and smash it flat with the palm of my hand.
Then I'd peel off the crust and toss them to Lady.

Somehow,
she always knew when I was making a sandwich.

*****

In first grade, I broke my arm.
My friend Chris and I were doing "Karate moves"
and "flips" during recess.
I couldn't flip very well.

I remember sitting in the office
and seeing lots of kids peer in through the door.
Since my parents were on a trip in Tennessee,
the school called Uncle Jon.

I remember the drive to the hospital;
Uncle Jon made sure to miss the potholes.
When we got there,
they fixed me up.
I don't remember it taking very long.

Uncle Jon took me to Aunt Judy's
(she's a nurse),
and I slept on the couch.
For a night or two,
she took care of me.
Once she asked,
"Would you like an ice cream sandwich?"
I hesitated in responding.
"No thanks."

(Who would put ice cream on bread?)

*****

Grandma and Grandpa would take each of their grandchildren (there are six of us) out to eat on their twelfth birthday.
Each of us had the choice of going wherever we wanted to go.
They also gave us twelve one-dollar bills.

I remember when Kristi and Lori each turned twelve, and thinking how I couldn't wait until it was my turn.

Finally the day came,
and I think we went to Russ' Restaurant.
(I remember going out to eat; I'm just not positive about where we went.)

About a year later,
my cousin Brian turned twelve and it was his turn.
I felt pretty old.

*****

I was on a T-ball team.
I was pretty good at it,
sometimes hitting doubles or even triples.
However,
the rules went that each kid on the team would be up to
bat only once,
then the other team was up.
Since I was always the last kid up to bat,
I never liked that rule.
No matter how well I did,
if I didn't hit a home run,
I was never able to score.
(It got better when the new kid joined the team.)

I also remember the first day I played softball
(on the Cub Scout team).
The pitcher threw the ball,
"Strike One!" hollered the umpire.

But I didn't even swing!

*****

Ka-Thump!

Every so often,
Aunt Pat and Uncle Jon would drop off Brian and Alison
to stay with us for a night or two.
(Sometimes I would stay at their house.)

One time when Brian was over,
he and I were playing in my room.
I was looking for something in the closet,
and Brian started climbing to the top bunk.
As soon as he got there and situated himself,
the entire top bunk crashed down to the bottom bunk.
Ka-Thump!
I spun around.
What I remember the most was the look on Brian's face.

I also remember I was glad I wasn't on the bottom bunk
at the time.

*****

I remember the night before my first day of sixth grade.
I was no longer going to be in elementary school.
Now I would be in middle school with other sixth,
seventh, and even eighth graders.
I was pretty restless that night
and had trouble getting to sleep.
When morning came,
I woke up before my alarm went off.
I went to the bathroom
and began getting ready for the big day.
I turned on the shower and was about to get in,
when there was a knock at the door.
It was Kristi.
"It's 3 a.m., go back to bed."

*****

Great Grandma was always happy to see me come over.

We'd watch wrestling on TV together,
and she'd often say,
"Now you can't tell me that doesn't hurt those guys."
Sometimes when Grandma and I would make an apple pie,
Great Grandma would peel the apples.
She would tell me about the days when she and Great
Grandpa lived in California.
A lot of the time she told me the same stories,
but I didn't mind.
Once,
she thought Kristi and I were married.
"Grandpa was a good man," she'd say.

Whenever we would invite her to our house,
"Ahh, all the hassle," she'd reply.
We would always manage to get her to come over though.

*****

For some reason,
I think I remember falling off the top of the slide on
the school playground.
I even think I remember feeling,
for a split second,
that I was flying.

As I try to think more about it,
it seems that falling off the top of a slide could really have
caused some injuries.
I don't remember any injuries though.

I guess I'm not too sure about this one.

*****

I remember I was in a play at church.
It was a Christmas play,
and my role was to be one of the sheep in the stable.

I did a pretty good job.

*****

There used to be a cement factory near our house.
(Now it's a bunch of stores.)
There were huge piles of rocks everywhere.
One day my friend Mark,
along with one of his friends and I,
decided to climb up them.

At one point,
I was on top of one of the hills,
and the guys were at the bottom of a hill nearby.
For some reason,
I picked up a rock;
it wasn't a big rock,
but it wasn't a small rock either.
I don't know why exactly,
but I decided to throw the rock near them,
thinking it would land somewhere near their feet
and scare them.
Well,
the rock hit Mark's friend square on the head.

Moral: Don't throw rocks.

*****

Z Z z z ~ ~ ... .

One Saturday morning,
as I was watching cartoons,
I noticed that my leg hurt.
No matter how I sat,
I couldn't get comfortable.
I told Mom when she woke up.
"You don't remember?" she asked.
"Remember what?"

Turns out,
during the night I had fallen off the top bunk.
Mom told me that the *thud* I made hitting the floor
woke them up.
I then ran around my room hollering,
"My leg! My leg!"

I guess I'm a pretty heavy sleeper.

*****

Dad once gave me a train set.
It wasn't just an ordinary set,
it was his when he was a kid.
He also gave me a big square piece of wood that was
covered with green carpet to set it up on.
It was a great train set,
no little wimpy train,
but solid, heavy train cars.
There was a black box with an on/off switch and a whistle.

One day when I was a little older,
Scott and his dad offered me fifty bucks for it,
and I sold it.

Today,
I sit and think about that decision.
I try to look through my father's eyes.
He let me sell it simply so I could have fifty bucks
to go waste on some new toy or game.
I wish I hadn't sold it,
but it's too late now.

I guess that's part of being a dad,
letting your children make poor decisions.

*****

I built a fort under the staircase in our basement;
I used some old burlap material that Dad got from work
for the walls.
It was a great fort.
It had a front room as well as a back one.
There were two entrances.
There was plenty of space.
It was huge!

The other day I looked where it used to be.
I didn't fit.

*****

I cannot fully articulate why these memories have lingered around in my head, while thousands of others are long forgotten. To the best of my knowledge, all of these memories actually happened, though a few of the details may be a little off. They are not in chronological order; instead, they are presented simply the way our memories work - jumping from here to there.

The idea for this book began while staying at my parents' house for a couple of nights during the Christmas season of 1998. Many memories ran through my head each night as I sat in my old bedroom and thought about my childhood.

I first made a list of anything I could remember as I sat in that old room. I walked around the house and looked through my box of old photos, letters, and junk. After I had a pretty good size list, I began elaborating on those memories by writing the first drafts. For a couple of months, I was quite excited about this project and worked on it whenever I could. Slowly, the idea was becoming a book and I was up to draft five. However, things became quite busy with the upcoming release of *The Tomato Collection*, and the idea was put aside.

Almost two years passed, and even though the idea was still rolling around in my head, I never really worked on the book of memories.

Then, in November, 2000, while visiting a middle school for a few days, I decided to bring out those rough drafts. The response from the students seemed to be pretty good, so I started thinking more about it. Not long later, however, the idea again went back to the filing cabinet.

It was July, 2001, when the motivation returned. I was talking about the idea with my fiancée, Stephanie, and we decided to work together and see if there really was any potential in this project. Picking up at draft five, we continued to drastically revise as I continued to think of more memories to add. Slowly but surely, the project was finally coming together.

We thought a lot about the design of the book and asked our friend Ryan to help with the cover and also to look over the poems. Between the three of us, countless changes were made until the final draft was ready.

That's basically the story on this book.

- Kevin
September, 2001

Copyright © 2001 by Kevin J. Kammeraad
All rights reserved.

Summary: A lighthearted, humorous, and sentimental collection of the author's childhood memories.

PUBLISHER CATALOGING-IN-PUBLICATION DATA
Kammeraad, Kevin J.
I remember : memories of growing up / Kevin Kammeraad.
— Grand Rapids, Mich. : Cooperfly Books, 2003, c2001.
  p.   cm.
ISBN 0-9669504-2-9
[1. Children's poetry. 2. Children—Juvenile poetry.]
I. Title.
PS3611.A564 A17   2003
811.008/09282—dc22   CIP

Printed in the United States of America

10 9 8 7 6 5 4 3 2

Editing: Stephanie Wenner
Art Direction/Typography: Ryan Hipp
Cover Design: Ryan Hipp & Kevin Kammeraad
Interior Design: Kevin Kammeraad, Stephanie Wenner, & Ryan Hipp
Book Production Coordinator: Tom Vranich
Photos: Steve Kammeraad

Cooperfly Books, Inc.
Grand Rapids, Michigan
1-877-9TOMATO
www.tomatocollection.com

For Grandma, Grandpa, and Grandma

Special thanks to: Stephanie, Ryan, Ron Oberbeck,
Becky Stanfield, Kyle Hofmeyer, Tom Vranich,
and all of my family and friends
(past and present).

About the Author:
Kevin and his wife, Stephanie, currently live in
Grand Rapids, Michigan. Kevin is the author and
illustrator of *The Tomato Collection* as well as the
producer of *The Tomato Collection* CD. Each year
Kevin and Stephanie travel to many schools sharing
their writing, music, art, and puppetry. Kevin is still
entertained by simple things.